*"Road Rage" is one driver expressing anger toward another driver. It is expressed with great intensity and in a felonious manner such as firing a weapon or assault. Road rage is a reaction to a perceived wrongdoing, disrespect or discourtesy in the other driver. The hostility is magnified by the stress of driving, and the personal stresses/issues the other driver brings with him/her into a vehicle."*

**Dr. Arnold Nerenberg**
"America's leading authority on 'Road Rage' and Aggressive Driving"

# ROAD RAGE
# JUSTIFIED

## 50 Rules Every Driver Should Follow
### (Black & White Interior Edition)

### NEVE ROARK

# PUBLISHER INFORMATION

Author website: www.RoadRageJustified.com
Author contact: comments@RoadRageJustified.com

Illustrations by Filipe Yuhoff

Publishing and Distribution: EBookBakery

ISBN 978-1-938517-67-9
Black and White Interior Edition

© 2017 by Neve Roark

ALL RIGHTS RESERVED

No part of this work covered by the copyright herein may be reproduced, transmitted, stored, or used in any form or by any means graphic, electronic, or mechanical, including but not limited to photocopying, scanning, digitizing, taping, Web distribution, information networks, or information storage and retrieval systems, except as permitted by Section 107 or 108 of the 1976 United States Copyright Act, without the prior written permission of the author.

# OVERVIEW

I consider myself pretty laid back, yet it's amazing how certain drivers set me off. Clearly I'm not alone.

I share the road with unconscious drivers who, at the least, make my trip less fun, or worse, make my travels unsafe. Since I see bad driving so often, my hope is that humor can help others see what they don't teach in driver's education. I see the need for a book on basic driving etiquette.

Take Road Rage. Who hasn't seen it? It is cited by the National Highway Traffic Safety Administration *(NHTSA)* as the leading cause of driving accidents. And while my title, *Road Rage Justified*, is tongue-in-cheek, Road Rage is real, dangerous, and terribly wrong. Yet, I'm convinced, if we follow certain rules and eliminate bad habits, aggressive driving will be minimized.

In the pages that follow you'll recognize familiar irritants. They're based on years of observation, and I'm betting you'll see your pet peeves too. Bad drivers come in *all* shapes and sizes and are present in every group.

# ROAD RAGE - BY THE NUMBERS

*"Inconsiderate driving, bad traffic and the daily stresses of life can transform minor frustrations into dangerous road rage," said Jurek Grabowski, Director of Research for the AAA Foundation for Traffic Safety. "Far too many drivers are losing themselves in the heat of the moment and lashing out in ways that could turn deadly."*

A significant number of U.S. drivers reported engaging in angry behaviors over the past year:

- **Intentional tailgating**
  51% (104 million drivers)

- **Yelling at another driver**
  47% (95 million drivers)

- **Honking to show annoyance**
  45% (91 million drivers)

- **Making angry gestures**
  33% (67 million drivers)

- **Blocking a car from changing lanes**
  24% (49 million drivers)

- **Cutting off another vehicle on purpose**
  12% (24 million drivers)

- **Getting out to confront another driver**
  4% (7.6 million drivers)

- **Bumping another vehicle on purpose**
  3% (5.7 million drivers)

Car crashes rank among the leading causes of death in the U.S., and what's more, nearly two in three drivers believe that aggressive driving is a bigger problem today than three years ago. Nine out of 10 believe aggressive drivers are a serious threat to their personal safety.

Aggressive driving and road rage varied considerably among drivers:

- Male and younger drivers, ages 19-39, were significantly more likely to engage in aggressive behaviors.

- Drivers living in the Northeast were significantly more likely to yell, honk, or gesture angrily than people living elsewhere.

- Drivers who reported other unsafe behaviors behind the wheel, like speeding and running red lights, also were more likely to show aggression.

Remember, you and I aren't the only drivers sharing the road, and our actions affect others more than we think. Don't be selfish or ignorant...**be aware** and we'll all make it home safely.

Thank you,
*An Average Driver*

# ROAD RAGE JUSTIFIED

## RULE #1

# LEFT-LANE CAMPER

The left (fast) lane is for passing. If you are determined to drive in this lane, move to the right if someone behind you is driving faster, regardless of how fast you're going. Driving the speed limit in the fast lane is not the answer.

**RULE #2**

# TAILGATING

Give the driver in front of you time to get the hint before you decide to ride their tail. If they don't move over, then just pass them. Tailgating will only lead to an accident.

RULE #3

# LANE CUTTER

We are all trying to get somewhere. You're not special. Get in line early and zipper merge appropriately.

## RULE #4

# FROGGER

Weaving dangerously in between cars to save yourself a few precious seconds is dangerous to you and everyone around you. If traffic is bad, pick a lane and stick with it until making a move makes sense.

**RULE #5**

# SOCIAL MEDIA ADDICT

Nobody cares as much about you as you.

Pause your social media agenda and focus on the road.

RULE #6

# PACER

Either speed up or move over. When you're in the fast lane driving the same speed as the car to your right, you eliminate passing options for those behind you.

RULE #7

# ENTITLED MERGER

When you're merging into another lane, remember you're the one merging. Do so with caution and at the same speed of the cars you're merging with so you don't cut anyone off.

RULE #8

## INTERSECTION STOPPER

When driving through an intersection, pay attention to the traffic flow. If the cars in front of you are stopped or slowing down, hang back so you don't get stuck in the middle of the intersection and block other cars when their light turns green. (You could also get a ticket!)

# RULE #9

# FREE-TURN BLOCKER

When there are two lanes at a stoplight and you are not turning right, stay in the left lane. This leaves a lane open for those who wish to make a free right turn.

RULE #10

# OBLIVIOUS BIKER

Unless you're able to consistently pedal faster than a car, stay to the side of the road. Why force the faster cars behind you to slow down?

RULE #11

# NO COURTESY WAVER

When someone is polite enough to let you into their lane, the least you can do is extend a courtesy wave. They didn't have to let you in, so show some gratitude.

**RULE #12**

# SUDDEN TURNER

If you're going to make a turn, remember your signal is to notify those around you of your intentions. Use it early. Not using it when you make a sudden turn only creates danger for those behind you.

RULE #13

# RUBBER NECKER

It's natural to be curious when you see an accident, but when you stop or slow down, it creates a ripple effect. This slows everyone down around you, even those cars coming from the opposite direction.

RULE #14

# BEAUTY DRIVER

If you need to put on your make up, do it before or after you are driving your car. Looking good isn't more important than being safe.

RULE #15

# GARBAGE DUMPER

Don't throw **anything** out of your window – enough said.

RULE #16

# CROWDER

When you park, center your car in the middle of the parking space. Be considerate of those who are also getting in and out of their cars around you.

RULE #17

# SHINER

Your brights aren't meant to be used when you're directly behind someone or a car is coming from the opposite direction. Don't be a dim bulb, use them wisely.

# RULE #18

# HANDICAP DISRESPECTER

Out of all the possible options, do you really need to take the only handicap spot available? There is a reason certain parking spaces are designated handicap and conveniently located in the front. Even if no spots are open, it's not yours to take.

## RULE #19

# LANE BLOCKER

If you find a parking spot and it's going to take a while for the driver to get in their car and back out, move over and put on your blinker. This allows cars behind you to pass. Making everyone wait until you are able to park is rude.

## RULE #20

# BUS PASSER

Buses aren't meant to be passed while they are stopped. That's why there are signs on the bus telling you this. Those getting on and off are often walking exactly where you want to pass...so be careful!

RULE #21

# CYCLE SPACE HOGGER

If you are riding your motorcycle and see available parking spaces designed for you, use them first. Leave the larger spaces for the cars.

RULE #22

# CROSSWALK BLOCKER

When you approach an intersection, make sure you're not stopping in the middle of it. This blocks pedestrians from safely crossing.

RULE #23

# THE BLIND PULL-OUT

If you're driving in a lane with slow moving cars and decide to switch to a lane with faster traffic, do so wisely. You don't want to pull out in front of someone who is driving fast and might not be able to stop.

RULE #24

# SPEEDER-UPPER

You had your opportunity to drive faster. If another driver is making their move to get around you, let them. It's not the time to speed up. Choose a speed and stick with it.

**RULE #25**

# ANTI-ZIPPER MERGER

When two lanes are merging, be considerate. Protocol is to follow an every-other order (a.k.a. zippering). Speeding ahead to prevent the merging car from getting in front of you is rude and inefficient.

RULE #26

# FAST-LANE TRUCKER

If you're driving a truck, stay out of the fast lane. It was never meant for you. The only reason you should ever be in it is to pass another car.

# RULE #27

# LANE SWEEPER

The left lane isn't a final destination for every driver. If you're going to sprint to get to the fast lane, first establish yourself in the lane you're currently in before merging.

RULE #28

# BLIND BACKER-UPPER

Backing out of a parking space quickly is never a good idea. Go slow. Look behind you. And remember, you're pulling into a lane where others might be driving by at faster speeds.

RULE #29

# NEIGHBORHOOD SPEEDER

Never drive over the speed limit in a neighborhood, and always be prepared to stop immediately. Just pretend they're your kids playing near the street.

RULE #30
___

## SLOW-MOTION MERGER

Merging is a moving process. It never involves coming to a complete stop, unless the cars in front of you trying to merge have stopped. Remember, there are people driving fast behind you. Slamming on your breaks or slowing down when you don't need to is dangerous. If necessary, use your entire lane and zipper merge appropriately.

RULE #31

# SPACE CROWDER

When turning into another lane, make sure there is enough space to do so carefully. Squeezing between two cars which are close together is not wise, especially at high speeds.

RULE #32

# ANTI-BLINKER

When you're going to switch lanes or merge, signal continuously (vs. a single, short blink) for at least 100 feet before making your move. This is especially true for those driving larger vehicles at high speeds.

RULE #33

# 4-WAY STOP CHEATER

When you are at a 4-way stop with cars waiting in multiple lanes, respect the pecking order and be courteous.

## RULE #34

# LANE CROSSER

If you need to make a turn, be sure you're in the correct lane when doing so. Cutting in front of cars to make a sudden turn can cause an accident.

RULE #35

# BRAKE TAPPER

Your brakes are meant to be used for stopping or slowing down. Using them all the time is dangerous and confusing to those behind you. (Not to mention bad for your car!) If you're consistently forced to brake because you're too close to the car in front of you, drive slower. Allow a safe space between you and the car you're following.

RULE #36

# CUTTERS

If you are turning in front of another car that has nobody behind them, why not wait a few extra seconds to avoid cutting them off. By letting them pass, you can safely turn into a wide-open lane.

RULE #37

# SOCIAL STOPPER

If you want to socialize with someone you see while you're driving, pull over and let the drivers behind you move on.

## RULE #38

# PRIVILEGED TURNER

There are certain turns you're not supposed to make. Nearby drivers expect you to follow the rules so they drive accordingly. When you decide to make an illegal turn, realize it can affect those behind you.

RULE #39

# DISTRACTED STOPPER

When you're stopped at a light, remember it will turn green eventually. So pay attention, and be ready to move ahead when the light changes.

RULE #40

# ROUNDABOUT CLOGGER

If you are entering a roundabout, yield to the traffic already in it. Don't come to a complete stop or slow down unless you are forced to. Roundabouts are designed to keep the flow of traffic moving.

RULE #41

# DOUBLE-LINE PASSER

Never cross a double line, especially critical when you are going around a corner or driving up a hill where oncoming traffic is not visible. There are reasons those lines are there.

RULE #42

# PARKING SPACE STEALER

If you come across an open parking space but notice another car waiting for it, move on and find another spot.

RULE #43

# PARALLEL PINNER

When you parallel park, make sure you're not blocking in other cars. Center your car between the other parked cars so they have enough room to maneuver and pull out.

RULE #44

# INVISIBLE DRIVER

Your lights are not only to help you see better, they help other drivers see you. This is especially true when it's dark and visibility is impaired. Make sure your lights are on at the appropriate times so you can be seen by others.

RULE #45

# DOUBLE-SPACE PARKER

When parking your car, be sure to use one space. I know your car is special, but taking up two spaces is never considerate.

RULE #46

# MERGE CHEATER

When you're behind a row of cars merging onto a freeway, don't cut over and speed ahead of them. Respect the pecking order, and focus on merging after you have established yourself in your lane.

## RULE #47

# DANGEROUS HAULER

If you're going to haul something behind you, make sure it's not going to fall off during transit and cause safety concerns for those behind you. Spend a little extra time tying everything down so it's secure.

**RULE #48**

# CALIFORNIA STOPPER

When you approach a stop sign, come to a complete stop before you move ahead.

RULE #49

## YELLOW LIGHT ACCELERATOR

Racing to beat a yellow light is dangerous. Yellow means to slow down and prepare to stop, not to race ahead.

RULE #50

# GAS PUMP MONOPOLIZER

When you stop for gas, pay attention to the space your car takes up. Don't block others from accessing their pump. By positioning your car appropriately, every pump can be utilized.

# AUTHOR'S NOTE

Why does bad driving set us off so quickly? I know there are many more noble causes to explore, and maybe I need to get a life, but I am amazed at the stupidity and recklessness I see everyday when I'm behind the wheel.

Through the years, I've observed drivers' bad habits and have come to the conclusion that regardless of age, socio-economic or educational background, ethnicity, culture, nationality, religion, race, or gender, the common thread is a large percentage of drivers who need to be clued in on what not to do. Driver's education at a young age is not enough and does not address what I call the "common sense" rules of the road. I understand I won't reach all drivers, so my hope is to make the roads safer, one driver at a time.

Perhaps I've missed a rule related to your own pet peeve? If I have, I'd like to hear your comments.

Let me know at:

www@RoadRageJustified.com

If you want to make the roads safer, buy a book for yourself and anyone you know who drives. Send a copy anonymously to that driver who could benefit the most.

Safe driving!

Order it from your local bookstore or online at:

www.RoadRageJustified.com
www.Amazon.com
www.BarnesAndNoble.com

www.ingramcontent.com/pod-product-compliance
Lightning Source LLC
Chambersburg PA
CBHW071715040426
42446CB00011B/2080